Internet safety

Stay safe on the Internet. Always ask an adult before you connect to the Internet. Follow our safe surfers guide on page 28.

Words marked in **bold** in the text are explained on page 32.

How to use this book
Look at the pictures in this book to find out what's happening on your computer screen.

Follow each numbered step in the book and on your computer.

1 Double-click on Internet Explorer.

Coloured arrows show you where to look on your computer screen.

Words that are underlined tell you what to do next.

What's the Internet?

The Internet is like a massive library, packed with information. In this book, you'll use your computer to explore the Internet.

A giant web

When you use the Internet, you share information with people in many different places. The Internet is often called the World Wide Web because it connects computers from all over the world, just like a giant spider's web.

Play and learn

The Internet has lots of uses. Here are a few of them. Can you think of more?

★ Finding information for homework or school projects.
★ Playing games.
★ Sending emails.

Pages to read

This is a website. It is made up of different pages, a bit like a book. But web pages are not made of paper. You read them on your computer screen!

Internet Magic

Claire Pye and Ruth Cassidy

W

FRANKLIN WATTS
LONDON • SYDNEY

This paperback edition
first published in 2004
Franklin Watts
96 Leonard Street
London EC2A 4XD

Franklin Watts Australia
45-51 Huntley Street
Alexandria
NSW 2015

© Franklin Watts 2003

Created by:
act-two
346 Old Street
London EC1V 9RB
www.act-two.com

Text: Ruth Cassidy
Consultant: John Siraj-Blatchford
Managing editor: Claire Pye
Editor: Deborah Kespert
Designers: Ariadne Boyle, Tim Clear
Illustrators: Ian Cunliffe, Andrew Peters
Art director: Belinda Webster
Editorial director: Jane Wilsher
A CIP catalogue record for this book
is available from the British Library.

ISBN 0 7496 5859 2 (pbk)

Printed in Hong Kong, China

Microsoft® Windows® and Microsoft® Internet
Explorer are registered trademarks of Microsoft
Corporation in the United States and/or other
countries. Screenshots reproduced with the
permission of Microsoft Corporation.

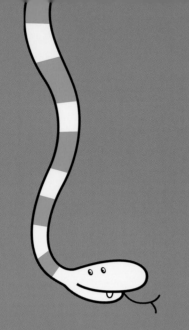

Contents

Find the address

Each web page has a different address, like this one. Most web page addresses begin with 'www', which stands for World Wide Web!

Internet Explorer

In this book, you'll learn about a **computer program** called Microsoft Internet Explorer, which helps you to read web pages and explore websites.

We've made up this website to show you how to explore the Internet. Ask an adult to help you find a website for you to explore. Then follow the steps in the book!

Wizard Websites - Homepage - Microsoft Internet Explorer

File   Edit   View   Favorites   Tools   Help

Back   Forward   Stop   Refresh   Home   Search   Favorites

Address   http://www.wizardwebsites/

Wizard Websites

Magic Links

History
Geography
Science
Art
English
Maths
Search

Search the Internet...

Go!

Find out how to make a cool compass on our Science Pages...

What's email?

Emails are a bit like letters, but you can send them in an instant!

Email stands for 'electronic mail'. No paper, envelopes or stamps are needed with electronic mail because information is sent directly over the Internet.

Outlook Express
In this book, you're going to learn about a **computer program** called Outlook Express. You can use Outlook Express to write email messages to your family and friends.

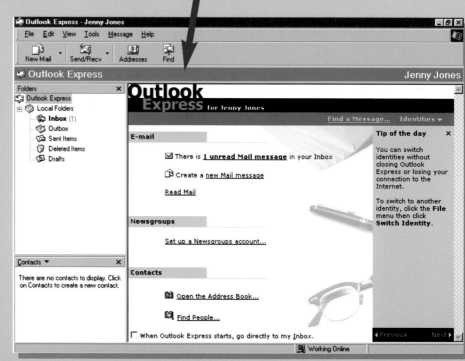

Instant messages

Email is a great way to share your ideas. You can work with a friend on a school project even when you're miles apart!

Decorate your email

There's a lot more to email than just words. You can decorate your emails, too!

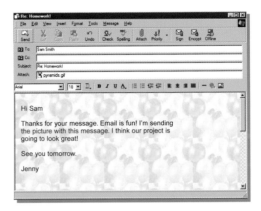

Mouse magic

When you move your mouse, a shape, called a **cursor**, moves around the screen. In this book, you'll need to move your cursor and click with your mouse. Here are the different ways of clicking.

Double-click
Press the left button twice, quickly.

Click
Press the left button on your mouse, once.

Right-click
Press the right mouse button, once.

Getting started

Let's open Internet Explorer and connect to the Internet!

1 Find Internet Explorer and double-click on it with your mouse.

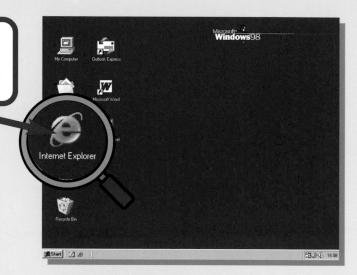

2 Don't worry if you see this 'Dial-up' box. It means your computer is connecting to the Internet. Just click Connect and it will disappear.

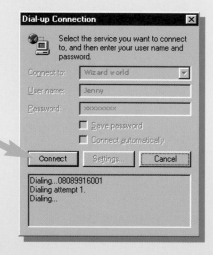

Hey presto!

Secret password

You might need a secret word, called a password, to connect to the Internet. If the 'Dial-up' box doesn't go away, ask an adult to tell you the password!

8

3 The first web page you see when you connect to the Internet is called your **homepage**. What does your homepage look like?

4 Internet Explorer has a **toolbar** filled with special buttons to help you explore the Internet.

Exploring different web pages and websites on the Internet is called 'surfing the Internet'. Check out our guide to becoming a safe surfer on page 28.

Explore a web page

Let's take a closer look at a web page and find out how to click on a **link**.

1 Most web pages are too big to fit on your computer screen. Look at the side of the screen for a bar like this. It's called a scroll bar.

2 You can move up and down the page using the arrows at the top and bottom of the scroll bar. Click on the down arrow to move down the page.

Hey presto!

Mouse wheel magic

Is there a wheel on your computer's mouse? If you have one, try turning it with your finger. It's a wizard way to whizz up and down a web page!

mouse wheel

3 Point your **cursor** at your web page and move it around. When the arrow turns into a hand, you've found a link!

4 When you click on a link, you jump straight to a different web page!

5 Links can be words, buttons, drawings or even pictures. Explore your web page. How many links can you find?

6 Now click on one of the links you've found to go to a new web page.

Back and forward!

Let's move from page to page using Internet Explorer's **toolbar** buttons.

1 We've jumped to a history page. What does your page look like?

2 Now, go back to the web page you were looking at before. Find this Back button on the toolbar and click on it.

Back

Forward Stop Refresh Home Search Favorites Media History

ww.wizardwebsites/history

Wizard Websites

Magic Links

Romans
Vikings
Egyptians
Incas
Aztecs
Greeks
Search

History Pages...

3 You went back, now go forward again! Click this Forward button.

4 It's easy to get lost when you're surfing the Internet! But don't worry, there's a quick way to get back to your **homepage**. Click on the home button now.

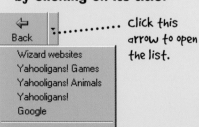

Search skills

Let's use the Internet to find information for a project all about pyramids!

1 Lots of web pages have a Search box to help you find exactly what you're looking for. Can you find a Search box on your web page?

2 First, click in the white box. Can you see a flashing black line?

3 Now, type the word 'pyramids'.

Search the Internet...

pyramids|

Go!

4 Finally, click the Go button to start your search.

5 Lots of **links** to web pages appear! They all contain the word you were searching for. <u>Click on one of the links now.</u>

6 With a little luck, you will have found just what you were looking for!

Did you find what you wanted straight away? If you didn't, go back and try clicking on a different link.

My favourite!

Let's find out how to save your favourite web pages so you can quickly find them again.

1 When you find a web page that you really like, click on the Favorites button.

2 A new list opens, here. Find this Add button and click it.

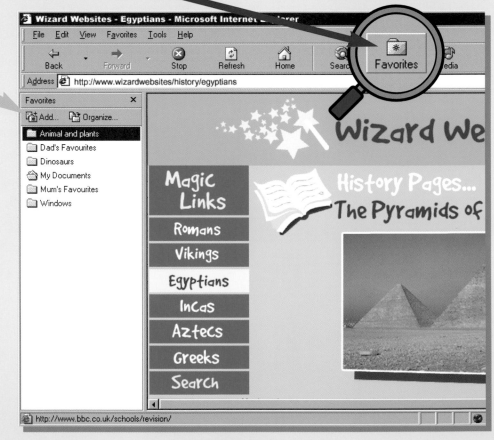

Wizard Websites - Egyptians - Microsoft Internet Explorer

File   Edit   View   Favorites   Tools   Help

Back   Forward   Stop   Refresh   Home   Search   Favorites   Media

Address   http://www.wizardwebsites/history/egyptians

Favorites
Add...   Organize...

Animal and plants
Dad's Favourites
Dinosaurs
My Documents
Mum's Favourites
Windows

Magic Links

Romans
Vikings
Egyptians
Incas
Aztecs
Greeks
Search

Wizard We

History Pages...
The Pyramids of

http://www.bbc.co.uk/schools/revision/

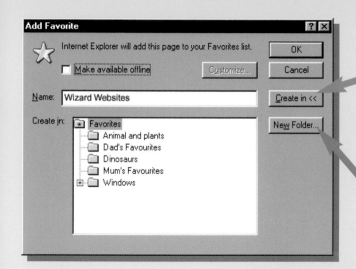

3 Does your Add Favourite box look like this? If it doesn't, click the Create in button to open a list of **folders**.

4 Let's make a folder to store your favourite web pages. Click New Folder.

5 Now type in a name for your folder. Why not try typing in your own name?

6 Click on the OK button to finish naming your folder.

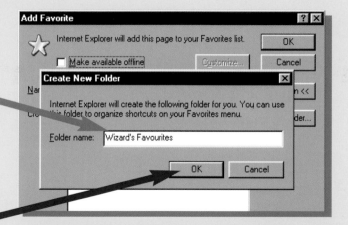

7 Finally, click OK again. Your favourite web page will be saved in your own Favorites folder.

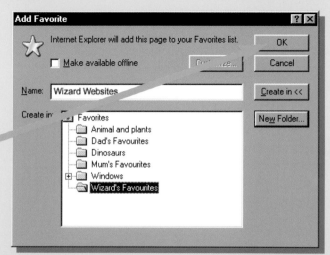

find your favourites

Jumping to your favourite web pages is easy
with Favorites. Let's find out how it works.

1 Start by going
back to your
homepage. Click
on the Home
button now.

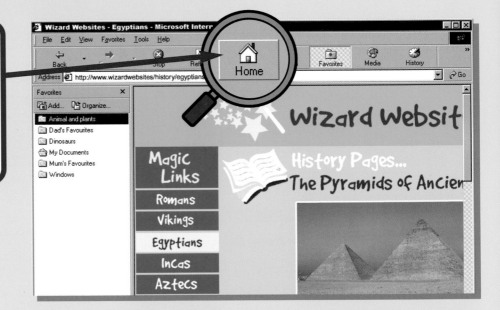

2 Let's find
your new favourite
page again. Find
the **folder** you
made on page
17 and click on it.

3 The web page you saved is safe inside the folder! Click on its name to jump straight to it.

4 Abracadabra! Your favourite page pops up!

5 Click the Favorites button again to close the list.

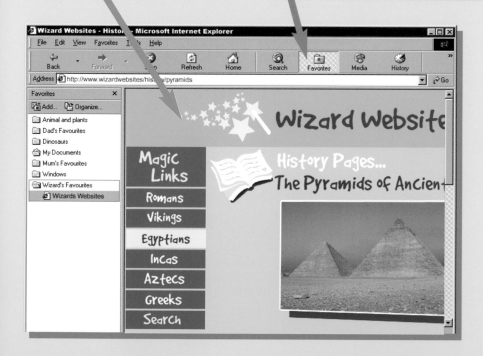

Don't forget to save all your favourite websites in your folder so they'll be easy to find later.

Save a picture

There are lots of great pictures on the Internet!
Here's how to save one for your homework project.

1 Find a picture and right-click on it. Just press your right mouse button, once!

2 A new list pops up. Move your **cursor** to 'Save Picture As' and click the left mouse button.

You can print pictures from the Internet, too! Click on Print Picture in the pop-up list.

Wizard Websites - Egyptians - Microsoft Internet Explorer

File   Edit   View   Favorites   Tools   Help

Back   Forward   Stop   Refresh   Home   Search   Favorites   Media   History

Address http://www.wizardwebsites/history/egyptians   Go

Wizard Websi-

History Pages...
The Pyramids of Ancie

Magic Links

Romans
Vikings
Egyptians
Incas
Aztecs
Greeks
Search

Open Link
Open Link in New Window
Save Target As..
Print Target

Show Picture
Save Picture As...
E-mail Picture...
Print Picture...
Go to My Pictures
Set as Background
Set as Desktop Item...

Cut
Copy
Copy Shortcut
Paste

Add to Favorites...

Properties

Internet

3 This My Pictures **folder** is the perfect place to store your pictures. It opens on its own!

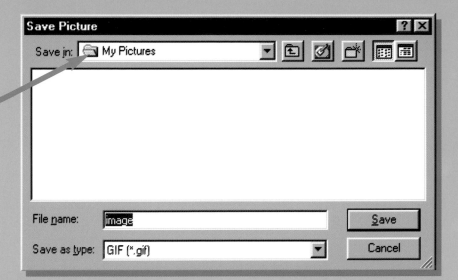

Save Picture

Save in: My Pictures

File name: image

Save as type: GIF (*.gif)

Save

Cancel

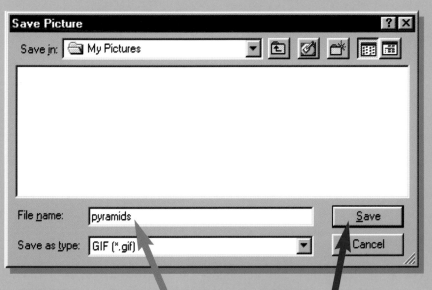

Save Picture

Save in: My Pictures

File name: pyramids

Save as type: GIF (*.gif)

Save

Cancel

4 Now type in a name for your picture. We've typed the name 'pyramids'.

5 Finish off by clicking on this Save button.

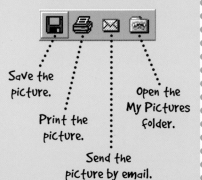

Hey presto!

Magic buttons
You can do lots of magic things with pictures. Move your cursor over a picture. Can you see these buttons?

Save the picture.

Print the picture.

Send the picture by email.

Open the My Pictures folder.

Open an email

It's great to receive email messages from your friends! Let's open an email and see what it says.

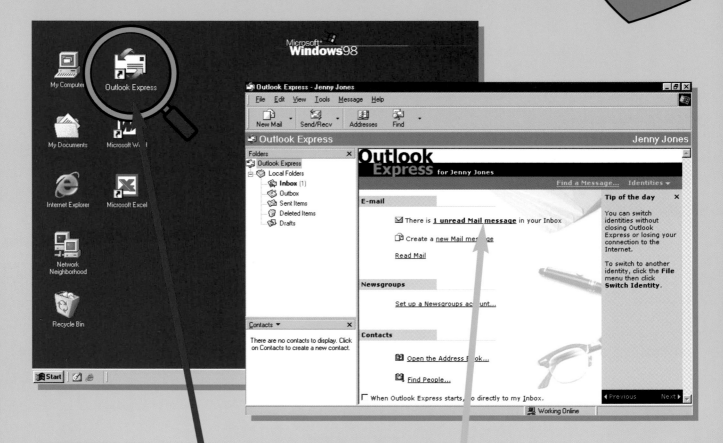

1 Find Outlook Express and double-click on it.

2 When you've got a new email, you'll see a message like this. Click on the message.

3 This is your **Inbox**. Can you see the new email? Double-click on the email to open it.

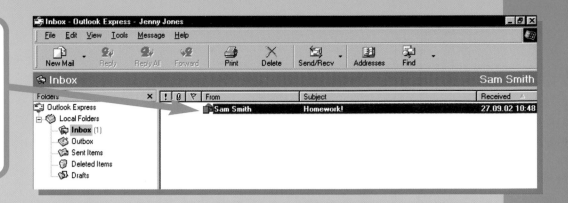

4 Here is the email. It's from Sam Smith.

5 You can see the date of the email here.

6 Sam tells you that the subject of his email is 'Homework'.

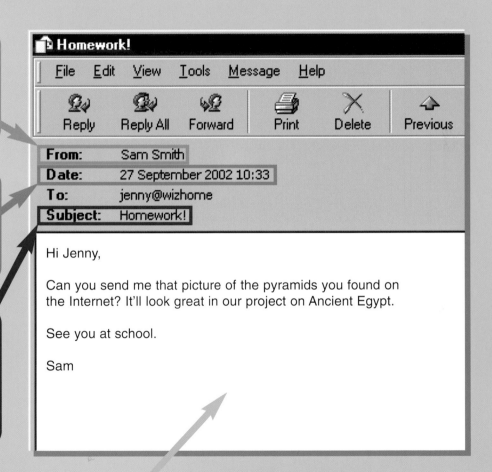

7 Now you can read Sam's email!

Reply to an email

It's time to write a reply to the email from Sam Smith. Here's how to do it.

1 <u>When you've read the email, click on Reply.</u>

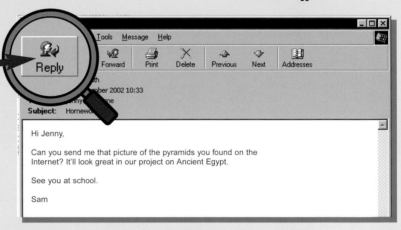

2 A new email appears and it's already addressed to Sam Smith!

3 The subject of the email is already filled in, too!

4 You can even see Sam's original email message.

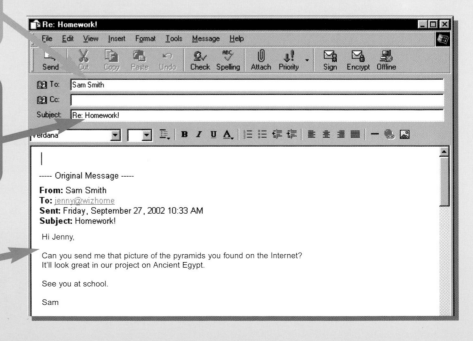

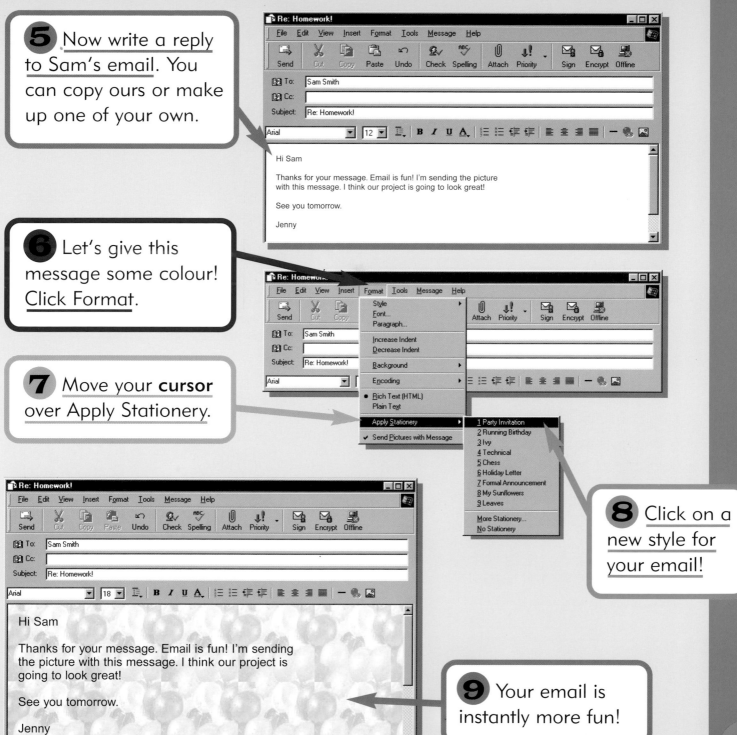

5 Now write a reply to Sam's email. You can copy ours or make up one of your own.

6 Let's give this message some colour! Click Format.

7 Move your **cursor** over Apply Stationery.

8 Click on a new style for your email!

9 Your email is instantly more fun!

Re: Homework!

File   Edit   View   Insert   Format   Tools   Message   Help

Send   Cut   Copy   Paste   Undo   Check   Spelling   Attach   Priority   Sign   Encrypt   Offline

To: Sam Smith
Cc:
Subject: Re: Homework!

Arial   12

Hi Sam

Thanks for your message. Email is fun! I'm sending the picture with this message. I think our project is going to look great!

See you tomorrow.

Jenny

Re: Homework!

File   Edit   View   Insert   Format   Tools   Message   Help

Send   Cut   Copy   Attach   Priority   Sign   Encrypt   Offline

To: Sam Smith
Cc:
Subject: Re: Homework!

Arial

Style
Font...
Paragraph...

Increase Indent
Decrease Indent

Background

Encoding

● Rich Text (HTML)
Plain Text

Apply Stationery

✓ Send Pictures with Message

1 Party Invitation
2 Running Birthday
3 Ivy
4 Technical
5 Chess
6 Holiday Letter
7 Formal Announcement
8 My Sunflowers
9 Leaves

More Stationery...
No Stationery

Re: Homework!

File   Edit   View   Insert   Format   Tools   Message   Help

Send   Cut   Copy   Paste   Undo   Check   Spelling   Attach   Priority   Sign   Encrypt   Offline

To: Sam Smith
Cc:
Subject: Re: Homework!

Arial   18

Hi Sam

Thanks for your message. Email is fun! I'm sending the picture with this message. I think our project is going to look great!

See you tomorrow.

Jenny

Attach a picture

Let's track down the picture we found on the Internet and send it to Sam in an email.

1 Click on the Attach button. It's the one with the picture of a paperclip.

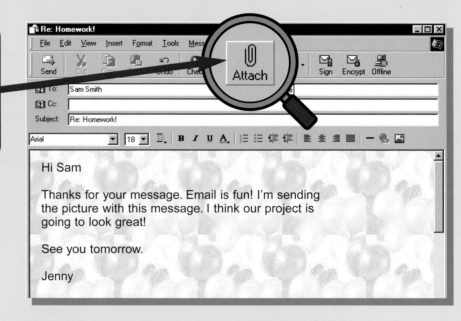

Hi Sam

Thanks for your message. Email is fun! I'm sending the picture with this message. I think our project is going to look great!

See you tomorrow.

Jenny

2 We saved our picture inside the My Pictures **folder**. Double-click on My Pictures to open it.

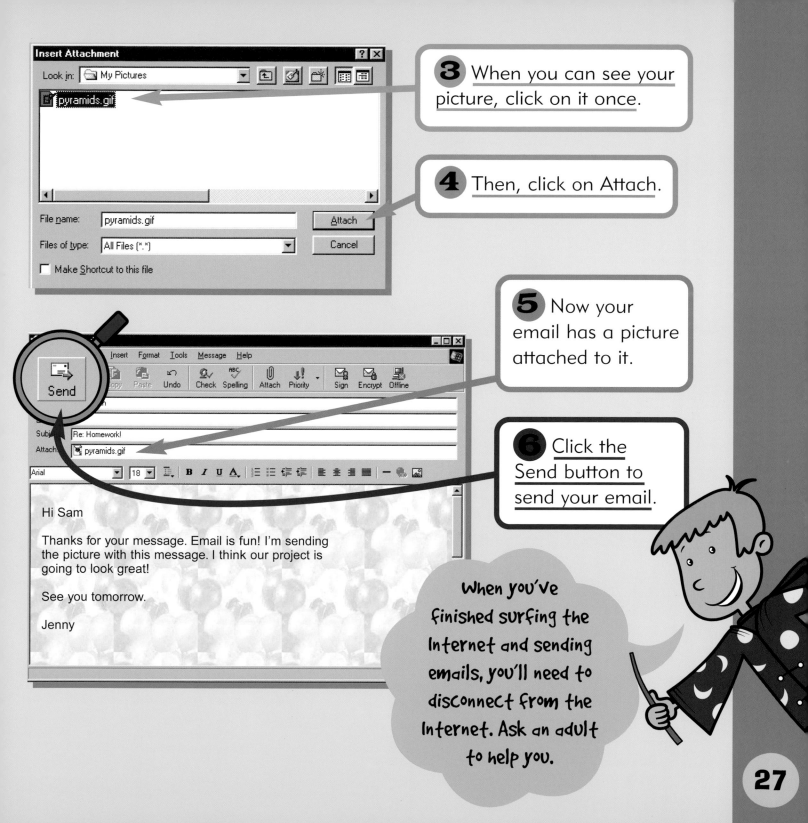

Insert Attachment

Look in: My Pictures

pyramids.gif

File name: pyramids.gif

Files of type: All Files (*.*)

Make Shortcut to this file

Attach

Cancel

3 When you can see your picture, click on it once.

4 Then, click on Attach.

5 Now your email has a picture attached to it.

Send

Insert Format Tools Message Help

Copy Paste Undo Check Spelling Attach Priority Sign Encrypt Offline

Subj: Re: Homework!

Attach: pyramids.gif

Arial 18 B I U A

Hi Sam

Thanks for your message. Email is fun! I'm sending the picture with this message. I think our project is going to look great!

See you tomorrow.

Jenny

6 Click the Send button to send your email.

When you've finished surfing the Internet and sending emails, you'll need to disconnect from the Internet. Ask an adult to help you.

Safe surfers

Now that you're an Internet and email wizard, read these tips for staying safe on the Internet.

Do

★ Do talk to your parents, teachers or other adults about using the Internet, and follow their advice.

★ Do tell your parents or teachers if you see or read anything that makes you feel uncomfortable.

★ Do ask your parents or teachers to help you find websites just for kids.

Don't

★ Don't ever give out personal information such as your address, email address, phone number or where you go to school.

★ Don't tell anyone your Internet password. It's meant to be a secret!

★ Don't reply to emails from strangers.

Remember these wizard web tips next time you surf the Internet!

Wizard website

Here's a cool website for you to explore.
It's called Yahooligans! and it's just for kids!

Loads of links
Click on these **links** to jump to other exciting Yahooligans! pages.

Search box
There's a handy Search box, just like the one on pages 14 and 15.

Time saver
Save time by using this Directory. It has links to thousands of great websites, all chosen by the Yahooligans! team.

What do you think?
Why not make your opinions count by voting in the Yahooligans! poll?

Guidance notes

This book aims to show children how to use the Internet and email safely and effectively. They also learn to search for information and share it with others.

Internet Explorer and Outlook Express
Both programs are part of Windows. All versions can be used with this book, although there may be slight variations in buttons and toolbars.

Macintosh users
Macintosh editions of Microsoft Internet Explorer and Outlook Express can be used with this book. Please note that mouse clicks are different, and buttons and toolbars may vary in appearance.

How to set up your computer

Children will find it easier to follow the steps if you set up your computer to look like the one in the book. Here's how.

Your desktop
Create Internet Explorer and Outlook Express shortcuts on the desktop.
1. Click Start on the taskbar and open Programs.
2. Right-click on Internet Explorer and drag it to a blank space on your desktop.
3. Select 'Create shortcut here' from the menu.
4. Repeat these steps for Outlook Express.

Outlook Express
Open Outlook Express and set it up as follows.
1. Click on Inbox in the Folders list.
2. Click the View menu.
3. Click Layout.
4. In the dialog box that opens, make sure that only the following are ticked: Contacts, Folder Bar, Folders List, Status Bar and Toolbar.
5. Make sure that 'Show preview pane', 'Show preview pane header' and 'Below messages' are all checked.
6. Finally, click OK.

Set up how Outlook Express opens
1. Open the Tools menu and click Options.
2. In the General tab, make sure there is no tick next to 'When starting, go directly to my Inbox'.

Connecting to the Internet
Children need extra guidance to connect to the Internet, especially if a password is needed.

Internet safety
Most schools and homes have systems in place to control Internet content. You can also enable Content Advisor in Internet Explorer. Here's how.
1. Click the Tools menu.
2. Click Internet Options.
3. Click the Content tab.
4. Under Content Advisor, click Enable, adjust the settings and choose a password.

Which website?

We created a dummy website for this book with all the features of a typical website. Here's how to set up the homepage of your choice.

❶ Find a suitable website for children.
❷ Click Tools and Internet Options.
❸ In the General tab, click 'Use current'.
❹ Click OK.

Extension activities

Each chapter of Internet Magic is self-contained so children can learn at their own pace. Hey presto! boxes contain tips and ideas for extra practice. There are more extension activities below.

Search skills

On pages 14-15, children search the Internet for web pages about pyramids. Ask children to search for other subjects. Brainstorm a list of 'key words' and experiment to find out how effective they are.

Fun with email

On pages 22-27, we open an email and reply to it. Do the same for your children. Send them an email similar to the one in the book. Alternatively, show children how to create a new email by clicking the New Mail or Create Mail button.

Make it fun!

Ask children about what they are doing and invite them to think about what they are going to do next. Encourage and praise them as they learn, and remember not to cover too much at once!

Health and safety

Supervise children when turning the computer on and off. Remind them not to put their fingers inside the computer. Encourage them to take regular breaks to avoid repetitive strain injuries and eyestrain. Refer to the computer manual for information about the correct seating and posture. Children should sit upright with their feet on the floor and the keyboard in line with their elbows.

National Curriculum links for Information and Communication Technology

Key stage 1

Finding things out
✔ 1a. Gathering information from a variety of sources. Developing ideas and making things happen.
✔ 2d. Trying things out and exploring what happens in real and imaginary situations.

Exchanging and sharing information
✔ 3a. Sharing ideas by presenting information in a variety of forms.

Key stage 2

Finding things out
✔ 1b. Selecting information for development using ICT.

Exchanging and sharing information
✔ 3a. Sharing and exchanging information in a variety of forms.

Breadth of study
✔ 5a. Working with a range of information to consider its characteristics and purposes.

Scottish National Guidelines 5-14 ICT

Strands covered at levels A and B
✔ Using the technology
✔ Searching and researching
✔ Communicating and collaborating

Useful words

computer program
A computer program helps you to do different jobs on your computer. In this book, we learn about programs called Internet Explorer and Outlook Express.

cursor
The cursor is what moves on screen when you move your mouse. You use it to point to different parts of your screen.

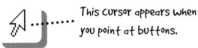
This cursor appears when you point at buttons.

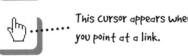
This cursor appears when you point at a link.

folder
A computer folder is used for storing work, just like a real folder. In this book, you find a picture on the Internet and store it in a folder called My Pictures.

 My Pictures

homepage
The first page you see when you connect to the Internet is called your homepage.

Inbox
The email Inbox is the place where all your new emails are stored, ready for you to read them.

link
You click on links to jump from one web page to another. When you move your cursor over a link, it turns into a hand shape.

toolbar
Every computer program has a toolbar along the top of it. The toolbar is full of buttons that help you to work on your computer.

This grey bar is a toolbar.

Index